LOW FAT COOKBOOK

Published by Tesco Stores Limited
Created by Brilliant Books Ltd
84-86 Regent Street
London W1B 5RR
www.brilliantbooks.co.uk

First published 2001

Text and photographs © 2001 Brilliant Books Ltd

Printed by Printer Trento, S.r.l., Italy
Reproduction by Colourpath, England

ISBN 1-84221-139-0

10 9 8 7 6 5 4 3 2 1

PICTURE CREDITS

Jean Cazals, Laurie Evans,
Christine Hanscomb, David Munns,
Thomas Odulate, Trevor Vaughan,
Philip Wilkins, Frank Wieder, Huw Williams

LOW FAT COOKBOOK

CONTENTS

HEALTHY, DELICIOUS AND LOW FAT

There are more than twice as many calories in fat as there are in carbohydrates or protein, which is why cutting down on fat is such a good way to lose weight. Many people also choose to eat less 'unhealthy' saturated fats – found in meat, biscuits, cakes, crisps, cheese and other dairy products – to reduce the risk of heart disease. Women should aim to have about 70g of fat a day, while men should have around 95g. The recipes in this book have less than 10g of fat per portion, yet they are all delicious. They prove there's no need for faddy diets and self-denial routines that are impossible to keep up. After all, fresh herbs and a squeeze of fresh lime juice add just as much flavour as a rich creamy sauce or a dollop of fatty mayonnaise.

USING THE RECIPES

1. Both metric and imperial weights and measures are given, except for goods sold in standard size packaging, such as cans. As conversions cannot always be exact, you should follow either the metric or the imperial throughout the recipe where possible. 2. British standard level spoon measurements are used. A tablespoon measure is equivalent to 15ml; a teaspoon measure is equivalent to 5ml. 3. Dishes cooked in the oven should be placed in the centre, unless otherwise stated. Tesco advises that all meat, poultry, fish and eggs should be cooked thoroughly. When cooked, poultry juices should run clear when the flesh is pierced with a skewer at its thickest point. 4. Recipes containing soft ripened cheeses, sesame products, nuts or nut derivatives should not be eaten by children, people who have an allergic reaction to nuts, or women who are pregnant or breastfeeding. 5. Vegetables and fruits used are medium-sized, unless otherwise specified. 6. The fat and calorie content of each recipe is given. These figures are for one serving only. 7. Each recipe has been given a simplicity rating of one, two or three chef's hats. One chef's hat means easy; two or three will require a little more effort.

ROASTED PEPPER AND TOMATO SOUP

Serves 4

Preparation 15 mins

plus 10 mins cooling

Cooking 35 mins

Calories 79

Fat 1g

Simplicity

1 Preheat the oven to 200°C/400°F/Gas Mark 6. Place the peppers and onion on a baking sheet, cut-side down, and add the whole tomatoes and garlic. Cook in the oven for 30 minutes or until tender and well browned.

2 Leave the vegetables and garlic to cool for 10 minutes, then peel them. Place the vegetables and garlic in a food processor with half the stock and blend until smooth, or use a hand blender.

3 Return to the pan, add the remaining stock and tomato purée, then bring to the boil. Season to taste and scatter over the parsley just before serving.

3 red or orange peppers, halved and deseeded

1 onion, unpeeled and halved

4 large plum tomatoes

4 cloves garlic, unpeeled

350ml (12fl oz) chicken or vegetable stock

1 tbsp tomato purée

Salt and black pepper

2 tbsp chopped fresh parsley

You can tell how good this soup tastes just by looking at it. Its flavour really is as fresh as its colour. Serve it with some crusty bread, warmed in the oven.

THAI HOT AND SOUR PRAWN SOUP

Simplicity 👨‍🍳 👨‍🍳

Serves 4

Preparation 25 mins

Cooking 30 mins

Calories 148

Fat 5g

2 stalks lemon grass

300g (11oz) whole raw shell-on prawns, defrosted if frozen

1 tbsp vegetable oil

1 litre (1¾ pints) chicken stock

1 clove garlic, crushed

2.5cm (1in) piece fresh root ginger, roughly chopped

Grated rind of 1 lime and juice of 2 limes

1 green chilli, deseeded and finely chopped

Salt and black pepper

1 tbsp Thai fish sauce

1 red chilli, deseeded and sliced, and 2 tbsp chopped fresh coriander to garnish

1 Peel the outer layers from the lemon grass stalks and chop the lower white bulbous parts into 3 pieces, discarding the fibrous tops. Shell the prawns, leaving the tails attached and reserving the shells for the stock. Cut a slit along the back of each prawn with a sharp knife and remove the thin black vein. Rinse the prawns, then refrigerate until needed.

2 Heat the oil in a large saucepan. Fry the prawn shells for 2-3 minutes, until pink. Add the stock, garlic, ginger, lemon grass, lime rind, green chilli and salt to taste. Bring to the boil, then reduce the heat, cover and simmer for 20 minutes.

3 Strain the stock and return to the pan. Stir in the fish sauce and lime juice and bring to the boil. Add the prawns and simmer gently for 3 minutes. Season and garnish with the red chilli and coriander.

This popular Thai soup, known as Tom Yum Kung, will set the taste buds tingling. It's got a wonderfully fragrant citrus flavour, which is followed by a real chilli kick.

MELON AND GRAPEFRUIT SALAD

Serves 4

Preparation 20 mins
plus 1 hr chilling

Calories 57

Fat trace

Simplicity

1 Cut the melon into segments and remove the seeds. Dice the flesh, or scoop it out using a melon baller. Place in a serving bowl.

2 Slice the top and bottom off each grapefruit and place on a work surface. Using a small serrated knife, cut off the skin and pith, following the curve of the fruit. Holding the grapefruit over a bowl, cut between the membranes to release the segments. Add the segments and juice to the melon.

3 Pour the orange juice and liqueur, if using, over the fruit and stir gently to mix. Cover and refrigerate for at least 1 hour before serving. Garnish with fresh mint.

1 medium or 2 small melons, such as galia, charentais, honeydew, cantaloupe or ogen

2 pink grapefruit

8 tbsp unsweetened fresh orange juice

1 tbsp orange liqueur, such as Cointreau or medium sherry (optional)

Fresh mint to garnish

If you want a light and refreshing starter, this is it. A dash of liqueur brings out the sweetness of the fruit and if you feel like it, add a few slices of Parma ham.

CHICKEN WALDORF SALAD

Simplicity

Serves 4

Preparation 15 mins
plus 1 hr chilling

Calories 230

Fat 9g

175g (6oz) cooked boneless chicken breasts, skinned and diced

4 sticks celery, thinly sliced

25g (1oz) walnuts, roughly chopped

1 red-skinned eating apple

1 green-skinned eating apple

Juice of ½ lemon

200g bag mixed salad leaves

Snipped fresh chives to garnish

For the dressing

1 tbsp reduced calorie mayonnaise

5 tbsp low fat natural yogurt

¼ tsp finely grated lemon rind

Black pepper

1 Place the chicken in a bowl, add the celery and walnuts and stir to mix. Core, then dice the apples and toss in the lemon juice to stop them browning. Add to the chicken and mix well.

2 To make the dressing, mix together the mayonnaise, yogurt, lemon rind and black pepper in a small bowl. Spoon over the chicken mixture and toss lightly to mix. Cover and refrigerate for at least 1 hour before serving.

3 Arrange the salad leaves on serving plates and spoon over the chicken mixture. Garnish with fresh chives.

With its fresh lemony dressing, this simple Waldorf salad makes a great starter. To turn it into a deliciously light main course, just serve it with some warm crusty bread.

MARINATED MUSHROOMS ON A BED OF LEAVES

Serves 4

Preparation 15 mins
plus 2 hrs marinating

Calories 103

Fat 9g

Simplicity

1 To make the dressing, place the oil, apple juice, vinegar, mustard, garlic, herbs and black pepper in a bowl and whisk with a fork to mix thoroughly.

2 Pour the dressing over the mushrooms and stir well. Cover and place in the fridge for 2 hours.

3 Arrange the spinach and watercress on serving plates. Spoon the mushrooms and a little of the dressing over the top and toss lightly to mix. Garnish with fresh thyme.

350g (12oz) mixed mushrooms, such as shiitake, large open, button and oyster, thickly sliced

100g (3½oz) baby spinach leaves

25g (1oz) watercress, thick stems discarded

Fresh thyme to garnish

For the dressing

3 tbsp extra virgin olive oil

2 tbsp unsweetened apple juice

2 tsp tarragon white wine vinegar

2 tsp Dijon mustard

1 clove garlic, crushed

1 tbsp chopped fresh oregano

Black pepper

Leave the mushrooms to absorb the flavours of the tangy mustard dressing, then pile them on to the spinach and watercress. Warm ciabatta goes well with this salad.

PAN-FRIED PORK STEAKS WITH ORANGE AND SAGE

Simplicity 👨‍🍳 👨‍🍳

Serves 4

Preparation 10 mins

Cooking 25 mins

Calories 240

Fat 6g

---

1 tbsp olive oil

Salt and black pepper

12 thin-cut pork loin steaks

300ml (½ pint) chicken stock

Finely grated rind and juice of 1 orange

2 tbsp dry sherry or vermouth

2 tbsp redcurrant jelly

2 tsp chopped fresh sage or 1 tsp dried sage

---

1 Heat the oil in a large heavy-based frying pan. Season the steaks, add 6 steaks to the pan and fry for 4 minutes on each side or until cooked. Remove from the pan and keep warm while you fry the rest of the steaks. Add to the first batch and keep warm.

2 Add the stock, orange rind and juice, sherry or vermouth and redcurrant jelly to the pan. Cook vigorously over a high heat for 5 minutes, stirring, or until reduced by half and darkened in colour.

3 Stir the sage into the sauce and season to taste. Return the steaks to the pan and heat for 1-2 minutes to warm through. Spoon over the sauce.

Orange cuts through the richness of the pork in this quick and simple dish. Serve on a bed of shredded cabbage with new potatoes and the sauce spooned over.

SPICED BEEF AND CARROT BURGERS

Serves 4

Preparation 15 mins

Cooking 15-20 mins

Calories 231

Fat 8g

Simplicity

1 Preheat the grill to medium. Place all the ingredients in a large bowl and mix together well.

2 Shape the mixture into 4 round flat burgers, using your hands. Grill for about 15-20 minutes, turning once, until the burgers are lightly browned and cooked through.

450g (1lb) extra lean minced beef

2 carrots, coarsely grated

75g (3oz) mushrooms, finely chopped

1 large onion or 3 shallots, finely chopped

50g (2oz) fresh wholemeal breadcrumbs

2 tbsp tomato purée

1 medium egg, lightly beaten

1 clove garlic, crushed

2 tsp ground cumin

2 tsp ground coriander

1 tsp hot chilli powder

Black pepper

These healthy burgers will be popular with all the family. Try serving them in granary baps piled high with crisp salad leaves, slices of tomato and tangy relish.

CHICKEN ROGAN JOSH

Simplicity

Serves 4

Preparation 15 mins

Cooking 1 hr

Calories 229

Fat 9g

Ingredients
8 skinless boneless chicken thighs
1 tbsp vegetable oil
1 small red pepper and 1 small green pepper, deseeded and thinly sliced
1 onion, thinly sliced
5cm (2in) piece of fresh root ginger, finely chopped
2 cloves garlic, crushed
2 tbsp garam masala
1 tsp each paprika, turmeric and chilli powder
4 cardamom pods, crushed
Salt
200g (7oz) low fat Greek yogurt
400g can chopped tomatoes
Fresh coriander to garnish

1 Cut each chicken thigh into 4 pieces. Heat the oil in a large heavy-based frying pan and add the peppers, onion, ginger, garlic, spices and a good pinch of salt. Fry over a low heat for 6 minutes.

2 Add the chicken and half the yogurt. Turn up the heat to medium and cook for 4 minutes, until the yogurt is absorbed. Repeat with the rest of the yogurt.

3 Increase the heat to high, stir in the tomatoes and 200ml (7fl oz) of water and bring to the boil. Reduce the heat, cover, and simmer for 30 minutes or until the chicken is tender, stirring occasionally and adding more water if the sauce becomes too dry.

4 Uncover the pan, increase the heat to high and cook, stirring constantly, for 5 minutes or until the sauce thickens. Garnish with coriander.

With its combination of Indian spices and creamy yogurt, rogan josh is a real winner. Serve it with rice, a cooling mint raita and some mango chutney.

CHARGRILLED CHICKEN WITH MANGO SALSA

Serves 4

Preparation 20 mins

plus 1 hr marinating

Cooking 20 mins

Calories 237

Fat 7g

Simplicity

1 Place the chicken breasts between cling film and flatten them with a rolling pin. Unwrap and put in a non-metallic dish. Combine the oil, fish sauce, lime juice and seasoning and pour over the chicken. Cover and leave to marinate in the fridge for 1 hour.

2 Meanwhile, make the salsa. Preheat the grill to high. Grill the pepper for 10 minutes, cool, then peel off the skin and dice. In a bowl, stir it into all the other salsa ingredients, season, cover and refrigerate.

3 Heat a ridged cast-iron grill pan over a medium to high heat. Wipe with the marinade, using a folded piece of kitchen towel. Alternatively, heat 1 teaspoon of the marinade in a heavy-based frying pan. Add the chicken and fry for 3-5 minutes on each side, until cooked through (you may have to do this in batches). Serve with the salsa, garnished with mint and lime.

4 skinless boneless chicken breasts

1 tbsp olive oil

2 tbsp Thai fish sauce

Juice of ½ lime

Salt and black pepper

Fresh mint to garnish and lime wedges to serve

For the salsa

½ red pepper, deseeded and quartered

1 mango, peeled and chopped

1 small red chilli, deseeded and finely chopped

1 tbsp olive oil

Juice of ½ lime

1 tbsp each chopped fresh coriander and mint

This spicy fresh mango salsa with sizzling hot chicken breasts is outrageously good. Try it with salad leaves, a squeeze of lime juice and new potatoes or rice.

MUSHROOM AND TARRAGON STUFFED CHICKEN

Simplicity

Serves 4

Preparation 30 mins

Cooking 40 mins

Calories 207

Fat 10g

2 tbsp olive oil

1 small leek, finely chopped

1 small courgette, finely chopped

1 clove garlic, crushed

50g (2oz) button mushrooms, finely chopped

50g (2oz) oyster or shiitake mushrooms, finely chopped

1 tbsp chopped fresh tarragon, plus extra leaves to garnish

Black pepper

4 skinless boneless chicken breasts, about 125g (4oz) each

1 Preheat the oven to 200°C/400°F/Gas Mark 6. Heat half the oil in a saucepan. Add the leek, courgette, garlic and mushrooms and cook for 5 minutes, stirring, until softened. Remove from the heat and stir in the tarragon and black pepper.

2 Place the chicken breasts between 2 large sheets of cling film. Beat to an even thickness with a rolling pin. Spread the stuffing evenly over each breast. Roll up, folding in the ends, and secure with wetted cocktail sticks. Brush with the remaining oil and place on a non-stick baking sheet.

3 Cook in the oven for 30-35 minutes, until the juices run clear when pierced with a skewer. Remove the cocktail sticks and cut each roll into 2.5cm (1in) slices, then garnish with fresh tarragon.

The aniseed flavour of fresh tarragon combines with chicken and mushrooms beautifully. Serve with new potatoes and fresh or roasted cherry tomatoes.

GINGER AND LEMON CHICKEN STIR FRY

Serves 4

Preparation 20 mins

plus 1 hr marinating

Cooking 12 mins

Calories 225

Fat 10g

Simplicity

1 In a non-metallic bowl, mix the lemon rind and juice, half of the garlic, and the coriander. Season with black pepper and add the chicken. Turn to coat, then cover and refrigerate for 1 hour.

2 Heat a non-stick wok or large frying pan and dry-fry the sesame seeds for 30 seconds, stirring. Remove and set aside. Add the oil to the wok or pan, heat, then stir-fry the ginger and remaining garlic for 30 seconds. Add the chicken and marinade and stir-fry for 4 minutes.

3 Add the carrots and leek and stir-fry for 1-2 minutes. Add the mangetout and bean sprouts and stir-fry for 2-3 minutes, until everything is tender. Pour in the sherry and soy sauce and sizzle for 1-2 minutes, then sprinkle over the sesame seeds.

Ingredients
Finely grated rind and juice of 1 lemon
2 cloves garlic, crushed
2 tbsp chopped fresh coriander
Black pepper
350g (12oz) skinless boneless chicken breasts, cut into strips
2 tbsp sesame seeds
1 tbsp sesame oil
2.5cm (1in) piece fresh root ginger, finely chopped
2 carrots, cut into matchsticks
1 leek, thinly sliced
170g pack mangetout
125g (4oz) bean sprouts
1 tbsp dry sherry
1 tbsp light soy sauce

The aroma of ginger, coriander and sizzling sauce will whet anyone's appetite, just make sure you don't overcook the vegetables – they should still be crunchy.

CHICKEN WITH SUN-DRIED TOMATO VINAIGRETTE

Simplicity

Serves 4

Preparation 10 mins

Cooking 15 mins

Calories 201

Fat 4g

4 skinless boneless chicken breasts

Salt and black pepper

2 tbsp balsamic vinegar

1 tbsp sun-dried tomato purée

175ml (6fl oz) dry white wine or chicken stock

1 tbsp olive oil

Large pinch of sugar

1 Place the chicken breasts between cling film and pound with a rolling pin to flatten slightly. Unwrap and season. Mix together the vinegar and tomato purée in a jug, then add the wine or stock, stirring to mix thoroughly.

2 Heat the oil in a large heavy-based frying pan. Add the chicken to the pan and cook for 5 minutes, turning once, then add the vinaigrette. Cook for 4-5 minutes, basting frequently and turning once more, until the chicken is cooked through.

3 Transfer the chicken to a board and slice diagonally. Cover and keep warm. Add the sugar to the pan juices and boil over a high heat, stirring vigorously, for 3-4 minutes, until reduced by half. Serve the chicken with the vinaigrette spooned over.

Here's an easy way to transform chicken breasts into something extra special, using just a handful of Italian ingredients. Serve with polenta and a leafy green salad.

TURKEY FILLETS WITH PARMA HAM

Serves 4   **Calories** 238   **Simplicity**

Preparation 20 mins   **Fat** 10g

Cooking 25 mins

1 Preheat the oven to 190°C/375°F/Gas Mark 5. Place the turkey fillets between sheets of cling film and pound with a rolling pin to flatten slightly. Unwrap the fillets, cut them in half widthways and season. Heat the oil in a large heavy-based frying pan, then fry the fillets for 2 minutes on each side, until they are seared.

2 Arrange the fillets in a single layer in a baking dish. Place 2 basil leaves on each fillet, then trim any excess fat off the Parma ham and crumple a piece over each fillet. Sprinkle over the Parmesan.

3 Add the wine or stock to the frying pan and bring to the boil, stirring, then spoon over the turkey. Cover with foil and cook for 15 minutes. Remove the foil and cook for a further 5 minutes or until the cheese is golden brown.

Ingredients
4 turkey fillets, about 100g (3½oz) each
Salt and black pepper
1 tbsp olive oil
16 fresh basil leaves
85g pack Parma ham
50g (2oz) Parmesan, freshly grated
75ml (3fl oz) dry white wine or chicken stock

If you like Italian food, you'll love this dish. Made with Parma ham, Parmesan and basil, it scores low on effort but high on flavour. Serve with some crusty bread.

FRAGRANT DUCK WITH PINEAPPLE

Simplicity

Serves 4

Preparation 20 mins
plus 20 mins marinating

Cooking 10 mins

Calories 203

Fat 9g

2 boneless Barbary duck breasts, about 175g (6oz) each, skinned and cut into strips

1 tsp five-spice powder

2 tbsp soy sauce

2 tbsp rice wine or dry sherry

1 tsp sugar

1 tbsp groundnut oil

1 orange or red pepper, deseeded and cut into thin strips

5cm (2in) piece fresh root ginger, cut into matchsticks

2 spring onions, white and green parts separated, thinly shredded

175g (6oz) fresh pineapple, cut into bite-sized pieces, plus juice

Salt

1 Place the duck, five-spice powder, soy sauce, rice wine or sherry and sugar in a shallow non-metallic bowl. Cover and marinate for 20 minutes.

2 Heat the oil in a wok. Remove the duck from the marinade and reserve. Stir-fry the duck over a high heat for 2 minutes. Add the pepper, ginger and the white spring onions and stir-fry for a further 3-4 minutes, until the pepper starts to soften.

3 Add the pineapple and juice and the marinade. Stir-fry for 1-2 minutes. Season with salt if necessary. Serve straight away, sprinkled with the green spring onions.

Fresh pineapple cuts through the richness of tender duck breasts marinated in Chinese spices. Serve this dish with plain boiled noodles or some fragrant Thai rice.

BAKED COD WITH GINGER AND SPRING ONIONS

Serves 4   **Calories** 114   **Simplicity**

Preparation 10 mins   **Fat** 2g

Cooking 25 mins

1 Preheat the oven to 190°C/375°F/Gas Mark 5. Line a shallow baking dish with a piece of lightly greased foil.

2 Place the cod in the dish, skin-side down. Pour over the soy sauce, rice wine or sherry, oil and salt to taste, then sprinkle over the white parts of the spring onion and the ginger.

3 Loosely wrap the foil over the fish, folding the edges together to seal. Bake for 20-25 minutes, until cooked through and tender. Unwrap the parcel, transfer the fish to a serving plate and sprinkle over the green parts of the spring onions to garnish.

Oil for greasing

500g (1lb 2oz) piece cod fillet

1 tbsp light soy sauce

1 tbsp rice wine or medium-dry sherry

1 tsp sesame oil

Salt

3 spring onions, shredded and cut into 2.5cm (1in) pieces, white and green parts separated

2.5cm (1in) piece fresh root ginger, finely chopped

One of the best ways to cook fish is to bake it in a foil parcel, so that it cooks in its own juices. Here, sesame oil, ginger and spring onions add a Chinese twist.

BAKED COD PARCELS

Simplicity

Serves 4

Preparation 15 mins

Cooking 30 mins

Calories 200

Fat 5g

1 tbsp olive oil

1 small onion, thinly sliced

1 clove garlic, thinly sliced

700g (1lb 9oz) skinless cod fillet, cut into 4 equal pieces

3 tbsp chopped fresh parsley

1 lemon, thinly sliced

4 plum tomatoes, each cut lengthways into 8 pieces

Salt and black pepper

4 tbsp dry white wine

1 Preheat the oven to 200°C/400°F/Gas Mark 6. Cut 4 double-thickness, 38cm (15in) square pieces of non-stick baking paper.

2 Heat the oil in a frying pan, then fry the onion and garlic for 2-3 minutes, until softened. Place a spoonful of the mixture in the centre of each square of paper. Top with a piece of cod, sprinkle over the parsley, then arrange the lemon slices on top.

3 Divide the tomatoes between the paper squares. Season, then spoon over the wine. Lift opposite sides of the paper up and bring them over the filling, then fold over firmly at the top to make a sealed parcel. Place on a baking sheet and cook for 20-25 minutes, until the fish is tender and cooked.

Cooking fish in parcels is easy – and because all the flavours are sealed in, the result is fabulous. You can really taste the wine, tomatoes, lemon and parsley.

MARINATED MONKFISH KEBABS

Serves 4

Preparation 25 mins

plus 2 hrs marinating

Cooking 15 mins

Calories 118

Fat 2g

Simplicity

1 Soak 4 wooden skewers in water for 10 minutes while preparing the vegetables. Thread equal amounts of the monkfish, onions or shallots, peppers and courgette onto each skewer.

2 Place the kebabs in a shallow non-metallic dish in a single layer. In a small bowl, mix together the lemon rind and juice, the orange juice, sherry, honey, garlic and black pepper and pour over the kebabs. Turn to coat all over, then cover and refrigerate for 2 hours.

3 Preheat the grill to medium. Grill the kebabs for 10-15 minutes, until the fish is tender, turning occasionally. Baste frequently with the marinade to keep the kebabs moist. Garnish with the fresh herbs.

400g (14oz) skinless boneless monkfish fillet, cut into 2.5cm (1in) cubes

4 small shallots, halved

1 small red and 1 small yellow pepper, each deseeded and cut into 8 or 12 chunks

1 small courgette, cut into 12 thin slices

Finely grated rind and juice of 1 lemon

2 tbsp freshly squeezed orange juice

1 tbsp dry sherry

2 tsp clear honey

2 cloves garlic, crushed

Black pepper

Fresh herbs to garnish

Monkfish is excellent for these kebabs because it has a firm texture and keeps its shape well. The only other thing you need to complete this dish is some steamed rice.

TANDOORI COLEY FILLETS WITH CUCUMBER RAITA

Simplicity

Serves 4

Preparation 15 mins

plus 2 hrs marinating

Cooking 20 mins

Calories 302

Fat 9g

2 tbsp hot curry powder

2 tsp garam masala

2 tbsp vegetable oil

2 tbsp lime juice

1-2 cloves garlic, crushed

1-2 chillies, deseeded and finely chopped (optional)

½ tsp salt

2 coley fillets, about 450g (1lb) each, skinned and each cut into 4 pieces

For the raita

2 tsp cumin seeds

1 cucumber, peeled, deseeded and thinly sliced or chopped

2 x 125g cartons natural yogurt

Salt and black pepper

1 Mix together the curry powder, garam masala, oil, lime juice, garlic, chillies, if using, and salt in a large non-metallic bowl. Add the fish and turn to coat. Cover and leave in the fridge for 2 hours, or overnight.

2 Preheat the oven to 220°C/425°F/Gas Mark 7. Place the fish in an ovenproof dish and cook for 15-20 minutes, until firm and cooked through.

3 Meanwhile, make the cucumber raita. Put the cumin seeds into a small frying pan and fry gently for 2 minutes to release their flavour. Mix with the cucumber and yogurt in a small bowl, then season to taste. Serve with the fish.

A pungent mix of spices turns this inexpensive white fish into an exotic golden treat. Serve with some warmed naan bread and a tomato and onion salad.

TAGLIATELLE WITH TOMATO AND MUSSELS

Serves 4

Preparation 20 mins

Cooking 30 mins

Calories 488

Fat 10g

Simplicity

1 To make the sauce, cover the plum tomatoes with boiling water and leave for 30 seconds. Drain, peel and deseed them and chop the flesh.

2 Heat the oil in a saucepan. Add the onion, garlic, celery, pepper and mushrooms and cook for 5 minutes or until softened, stirring occasionally. Mix in the chopped tomatoes and the rest of the ingredients for the sauce. Bring to the boil, cover, then reduce the heat and simmer for 20 minutes or until the vegetables are tender, stirring occasionally.

3 Meanwhile, cook the tagliatelle according to the packet instructions. Stir the mussels into the tomato sauce and season to taste. Increase the heat slightly and cook, uncovered, for 5 minutes, stirring occasionally. Drain the pasta and stir it into the sauce with the basil. Garnish with the extra basil leaves.

350g (12oz) dried tagliatelle

225g (8oz) cooked shelled mussels

2 tbsp chopped fresh basil, plus whole leaves to garnish

For the sauce

700g (1lb 9oz) plum tomatoes

1 tbsp olive oil

1 onion, finely chopped

2 cloves garlic, finely chopped

2 sticks celery, finely chopped

1 red pepper, deseeded and finely chopped

125g (4oz) mushrooms, chopped

4 sun-dried tomatoes, soaked, drained and finely chopped

6 tbsp red wine

2 tbsp tomato purée

This homemade mussel and fresh tomato sauce is both quick to make and scrumptious to eat. If you don't want to use any alcohol, you can use apple juice instead of wine.

THAI-STYLE SHELLFISH AND POMELO SALAD

Simplicity

Serves 4

Preparation 30 mins

plus 5 mins cooling

Cooking 3 mins

Calories 156

Fat 5g

1 pomelo or 2 pink grapefruit

200g (7oz) cooked
peeled prawns

170g can crabmeat in
brine, drained

1 Little Gem lettuce, chopped

1 spring onion, finely chopped

For the dressing

1 tbsp groundnut oil

1 clove garlic, finely chopped

1 shallot, finely chopped

1 red chilli, deseeded and
finely chopped

2 tbsp Thai fish sauce

2 tbsp soft dark brown sugar

Juice of 1 lime

1 First make the dressing. Heat the oil in a small frying pan. Fry the garlic, shallot and chilli for 3 minutes or until the garlic has turned pale golden and the shallot has softened. Mix together the fish sauce, sugar and lime juice, stir in the shallot mixture, then set aside for 5 minutes to cool.

2 Using a sharp knife, slice off the top and bottom of the pomelo or grapefruit, then remove the skin and pith, following the curve of the fruit. Cut between the membranes to release the segments.

3 Mix the pomelo or grapefruit segments with the prawns, crabmeat and lettuce. Pour over the dressing and toss, then sprinkle over the spring onion.

Pomelos look like grapefruit but have a sweeter flesh. If you can't get them, use pink grapefruit which go just as well with the crab and prawns in this fresh, light salad.

TIGER PRAWN, MANGO AND MANGETOUT STIR FRY

Serves 4

Preparation 15 mins

Cooking 5 mins

Calories 221

Fat 7g

Simplicity

1 Cut a slit along the back of each prawn with a sharp knife and remove any thin black vein.

2 Heat the oil in a wok, add the ginger and prawns and stir-fry for 2 minutes or until the prawns are just turning pink. Add the mangetout and spring onions and stir-fry for a further minute to soften slightly. Stir in the mango and soy sauce and stir-fry for 1 minute to heat through.

Ingredients
2 x 200g packs raw peeled tiger prawns, defrosted if frozen, rinsed and dried
2 tbsp vegetable oil
1½ tbsp finely grated fresh root ginger
300g pack mangetout
Bunch of spring onions, sliced
1 large ripe mango, peeled and thinly sliced
2 tbsp light soy sauce

Succulent prawns, crunchy mangetout and juicy mango are flavoured with soy sauce and fresh ginger. Best of all, you can get this dish on the table in 20 minutes. Serve with rice.

SPICY VEGETABLE COUSCOUS

Simplicity

Serves 4

Preparation 25 mins

Cooking 30 mins

Calories 406

Fat 9g

3 plum tomatoes

25g (1oz) butter

1 large onion, sliced lengthways

2 carrots, cut in half lengthways, then sliced diagonally

2 sticks celery, sliced

300g (11oz) pumpkin, deseeded, or swede, cut into 2cm (¾in) cubes

1 green pepper, deseeded and chopped

½ tsp dried crushed chillies

300ml (½ pint) vegetable stock

400g (14oz) couscous

400g can chickpeas or broad beans, drained

Salt and black pepper

1 Place the tomatoes in a bowl and cover with boiling water. Leave for 30 seconds, then peel and roughly chop.

2 Melt the butter in a large saucepan and fry the onion, carrots, celery, pumpkin or swede and pepper for 3-4 minutes, stirring, until softened. Add the chilli and tomatoes, cover and cook for 5 minutes, shaking the pan occasionally. Add the stock, cover and simmer for 20 minutes or until all the vegetables are tender.

3 Meanwhile, prepare the couscous according to the packet instructions. Stir the chickpeas or broad beans into the vegetables, season, then simmer for 5 minutes or until warmed through. Serve the vegetables piled on top of the couscous.

The fluffy texture of couscous helps it to soak up the rich vegetable stock in this dish. If you like, throw in some raisins and a sprinkling of cinnamon for sweetness.

PUMPKIN, LEMON AND PARMESAN RISOTTO

Serves 4

Preparation 20 mins

Cooking 35 mins

Calories 541

Fat 9g

Simplicity

1 Bring 300ml (½ pint) of the stock to the boil, then take the pan off the heat and stir in the saffron.

2 Heat the oil and butter in a large heavy-based pan and gently fry the onion and garlic for 4-5 minutes, until softened but not browned. Add the rice and pumpkin or squash to the pan, and stir for 2 minutes or until the rice is coated with oil.

3 Stir in the wine and boil for a few seconds to cook off the alcohol. Stir in the saffron stock. Simmer, stirring constantly, for 5 minutes or until the stock has been absorbed. Add half the remaining stock and cook, stirring, for 10 minutes, until absorbed. Add the remaining stock and cook, stirring, for another 10 minutes, until the rice is tender. Season to taste.

4 Stir the lemon rind and juice and the Parmesan into the risotto, then garnish with rosemary.

1 litre (1 ¾ pints) chicken or vegetable stock
Large pinch of saffron threads
1 tbsp olive oil
15g (½oz) butter
1 onion, chopped
1 clove garlic, finely chopped
400g (14oz) Italian risotto rice
1kg (2lb 4oz) pumpkin or butternut squash, deseeded and cut into 2cm (¾in) pieces
150ml (¼ pint) dry white wine
Salt and black pepper
Grated rind and juice of 1 lemon
25g (1oz) Parmesan, grated
½ tsp finely chopped fresh rosemary to garnish

Lemon cuts through the creamy richness of pumpkin in this risotto and heightens all the flavours. If you're not keen on saffron, try a pinch of turmeric or nutmeg instead.

PASTA PRIMAVERA

Simplicity

Serves 4

Preparation 25 mins

Cooking 20 mins

Calories 442

Fat 6.6g

1 tbsp sunflower oil

225g bag baby spinach

500g (1lb 2oz) broad beans (unshelled weight), shelled

500g (1lb 2oz) fresh peas (weighed in their pods), shelled

250g bunch asparagus, trimmed and cut into small pieces

125g (4oz) green beans, halved

6 tbsp low-fat yogurt

1 bunch spring onions, finely sliced

1 tbsp finely chopped tarragon, plus extra for garnish

Salt and black pepper

350g (12oz) dried penne pasta

1 Heat the oil in a saucepan, add the spinach, cover and cook for 5 minutes or until the leaves wilt. Set aside to cool. Cook the broad beans and asparagus in a little boiling water for 3 minutes, then add the peas and green beans and cook for 2 minutes or until tender, then drain.

2 Blend the spinach and low fat yogurt to a purée in a food processor or with a hand blender. Return the purée to the pan and stir in the drained vegetables. Mix in the spring onion, tarragon and seasoning and keep warm over a low heat.

3 Meanwhile, cook the pasta in boiling, salted water according to the packet instructions, until tender but still firm to the bite. Drain, then toss with the spinach and garnish with extra tarragon.

You can use any lightly cooked vegetables or pasta shapes in this springtime dish, but the green shades of spinach, peas, and asparagus are particularly pretty.

FRESH PASTA WITH TOMATO SAUCE

Serves 4

Preparation 10 mins

Cooking 15 mins

Calories 456

Fat 9g

Simplicity

1 Heat the oil in a medium-sized heavy-based saucepan over a medium heat. Add the onion and cook, stirring from time to time, for 2 minutes or until slightly softened. Add the garlic and cook, stirring occasionally, for 3 minutes or until the onion is tender but not brown.

2 Add the tomatoes to the pan with the sugar and bay leaf. Bring to the boil and season with salt and pepper. Reduce the heat, partly cover the pan and simmer, stirring occasionally, for 10 minutes, until the sauce has thickened. Remove the bay leaf.

3 Meanwhile, bring a large saucepan of water to the boil. Add 1 tablespoon of salt, then the pasta and cook according to the instructions on the packet, until the pasta is tender but still firm to the bite. Drain and serve with the sauce poured over.

500g pack fresh tagliatelle

For the tomato sauce

2 tbsp vegetable or olive oil

1 medium onion, peeled and chopped

2 cloves garlic, peeled and finely chopped

2 x 400g cans chopped tomatoes

1 tsp sugar

1 bay leaf

Salt and black pepper

This recipe may be simple but it is delicious and incredibly versatile. Adding some chopped chillis and a slug (or two) of vodka will transform it into a spicy arrabiata sauce!

VEGETABLE STIR FRY WITH HONEY AND MUSTARD

Simplicity

Serves 4

Preparation 25 mins

Cooking 10 mins

Calories 157

Fat 6.8g

2 tbsp sunflower oil

2 garlic cloves, crushed

225g (8 oz) broccoli, cut into small florets

1 yellow pepper, 1 red pepper and 1 orange pepper, deseeded and chopped

125g (4 oz) mangetout, halved lengthways

1 bunch spring onions, thinly sliced diagonally

juice of 1 lime

For the sauce

3 tbsp soy sauce

1 tbsp French mustard

2 tbsp honey

1 Make the sauce by mixing together the soy sauce, mustard, honey and 1 tbsp water.

2 Heat the oil in a wok or large frying pan until very hot. Add the garlic and broccoli and stir-fry for about 2-3 minutes or until softened. Add the peppers and stir-fry for a further 2-3 minutes. Add the mangetout and continue to cook for 1 minute.

3 Add the sauce and stir in the spring onions, then stir-fry for 3-4 minutes. Squeeze over the lime juice and serve with freshly cooked rice.

As the honey, mustard and soy sauce heat up, their flavours fuse into something magical. If you want to, try adding some fresh coriander or a little grated ginger.

CHILLI MUSHROOM STIR FRY WITH NOODLES

Serves 4

Preparation 10 mins

plus 15 mins soaking

Cooking 10 mins

Calories 188

Fat 8g

Simplicity

1 Cover the dried mushrooms with 75ml (3fl oz) of boiling water and soak for 15 minutes or until softened. Strain and reserve the liquid, then slice the mushrooms. Meanwhile, cook the noodles according to the packet instructions, until tender but still firm to the bite, then drain.

2 Heat the oil in a wok or large frying pan until smoking, then add the garlic, chilli and ginger and stir-fry for 15 seconds or until they release their flavours. Add all the mushrooms and stir-fry for 2 minutes or until softened.

3 Add the spring onions, sake or sherry, soy sauce, lemon juice, sugar, coriander, reserved soaking liquid from the mushrooms and the noodles, and heat for 1-2 minutes, until warmed through.

15g (½oz) dried porcini mushrooms

200g (7oz) fresh Chinese noodles

2 tbsp sunflower oil

4 cloves garlic, sliced

1 red chilli, deseeded and chopped

2 tsp ready-made ginger purée or finely grated fresh ginger

450g (1lb) mixed fresh mushrooms, quartered or sliced

4 spring onions, sliced

4 tbsp sake or dry sherry

4 tbsp dark soy sauce

2 tbsp lemon juice

1 tbsp sugar, or to taste

2 tbsp chopped fresh coriander

The chilli adds extra bite to this oriental mushroom and ginger stir fry. Sake is Japanese rice wine; if you haven't got any, you can use dry sherry instead.

VEGETABLE CHILLI BAKE

Simplicity 👨‍🍳 👨‍🍳

Serves 4
Preparation 25 mins
Cooking 1 hr 15 mins

Calories 197
Fat 5g

1 tbsp sunflower oil
1 onion, chopped
1 pepper, deseeded and diced
2 cloves garlic, finely chopped
1 chilli, deseeded and chopped
2 tsp ground cumin
1 tsp hot chilli powder
400g can chopped tomatoes
1 tbsp tomato purée
3 carrots, cubed
175g (6oz) swede, cubed
175g (6oz) mushrooms, chopped
3 sticks celery, chopped
6 tbsp vegetable stock
420g can kidney beans, drained
Fresh coriander to garnish
Salt and black pepper

1 Preheat the oven to 180°C/350°F/Gas Mark 4. Heat the oil in a large flameproof and ovenproof casserole dish. Add the onion, green pepper, garlic and green chilli and cook for 5 minutes or until softened, stirring occasionally.

2 Add the cumin and chilli powder and cook gently for 1 minute to release the flavours, stirring. Mix in the tomatoes, tomato purée, carrots, swede, mushrooms, celery, stock and season.

3 Cover and cook in the oven for 45 minutes, stirring once. Add the kidney beans, cover again and cook for a further 15-20 minutes or until all the vegetables are tender. Garnish with fresh coriander.

You'll tempt all your friends with these spicy vegetables piled into warmed taco shells. If you want, you can grate a little half-fat Cheddar on top and still feel virtuous.

THREE BEAN RICE SALAD

Serves 4 **Calories** 372 **Simplicity**

Preparation 15 mins **Fat** 6g

Cooking 40 mins

1 Cook the rice according to the packet instructions and until tender. Meanwhile, cook the baby broad beans in a saucepan of boiling water for 4-5 minutes, until tender. Rinse under cold water and drain, then remove the skins if you want. Rinse the rice under cold water, drain and place in a salad bowl.

2 To make the dressing, place the tomato juice, olive oil, vinegar, mustard, garlic, coriander and black pepper in a small bowl and whisk together until thoroughly mixed.

3 Pour the dressing over the rice and stir to mix well. Add the broad beans, black-eye beans, kidney beans, pepper and spring onions and mix well. Cover and refrigerate before serving. Garnish with fresh coriander.

225g (8oz) brown rice

175g (6oz) frozen broad beans

300g can black-eye beans, drained and rinsed

220g can kidney beans, drained

1 pepper, deseeded and diced

1 bunch spring onions, chopped

Fresh coriander to garnish

For the dressing

150ml (¼ pint) tomato juice

1 tbsp olive oil

1 tbsp white wine vinegar

2 tsp Dijon mustard

1 clove garlic, crushed

2 tbsp chopped fresh coriander

Black pepper

It's the tomato dressing which really makes this brown rice and bean salad taste so good. If you want to serve it warm, rinse the rice in boiling water before dressing it.

CARAMELISED BANANA PANCAKES

Simplicity

Serves 4

Preparation 10 mins

Cooking 25 mins

Calories 250

Fat 10g

1 large egg

100g (3½oz) plain flour, sifted

Pinch of salt

250ml (9fl oz) half-fat milk

25g (1oz) butter, melted

Sunflower oil for greasing

2 large, firm bananas, sliced

3 tbsp Madeira, dessert wine or 2 tbsp Drambuie

2-3 tsp demerara sugar

1 Beat the egg, flour, salt and a little milk to a smooth paste. Gradually mix in the remaining milk, then stir in the melted butter.

2 Brush a non-stick, medium-sized frying pan with the oil and heat until very hot. Pour in 2-3 tablespoons of batter, swirling to cover the base of the pan. Cook the pancakes for 1-2 minutes on each side, until golden. Repeat to make 7 more, keeping the pancakes warm and layering them between sheets of baking paper to stop them sticking.

3 Preheat the grill to high. Wipe the pan, add the bananas and alcohol and heat, stirring gently.

4 When most of the liquid has evaporated, spoon the banana mixture on to each pancake, fold it into quarters and place in a flameproof dish. Sprinkle with the sugar and grill until golden and caramelised.

These pancakes filled with hot gooey bananas have a hidden kick! For children, you can replace the alcohol with maple syrup. Serve with some low fat ice cream.

SUMMER FRUIT COMPOTE WITH VANILLA YOGURT

Serves 4

Preparation 20 mins

plus 15 mins cooling

Cooking 8 mins

Calories 191

Fat 5g

Simplicity

1 To make the vanilla yogurt, scrape the seeds from the vanilla pod into the yogurt and stir in the honey. Cover and refrigerate while you make the compote.

2 Put the berries into a saucepan with the port, sugar, orange rind and juice and the mixed spice. Heat for 5-8 minutes, until the fruit is just softened. Remove from the heat and set aside for 15 minutes to cool slightly. Serve the warm compote with a spoonful of vanilla yogurt.

675g (1lb 8oz) mixed summer berries, hulled or stalks removed and defrosted if frozen

75ml (3fl oz) port

50g (2oz) caster sugar

2 strips orange rind

Juice of 1 orange

1 tsp ground mixed spice

For the vanilla yogurt

1 vanilla pod, split

200g (7oz) Greek yogurt

1 tbsp clear honey

Thick vanilla yogurt made with clear honey has a real Mediterranean flavour, and tastes fabulous with this warm summer fruit compote. Serve with dessert biscuits.

WATERMELON WITH LIME SYRUP

Simplicity

Serves 4

Preparation 15 mins

plus 20 mins cooling

Cooking 5 mins

Calories 71

Fat 1g

Grated rind and juice of 1 lime

25g (1oz) caster sugar

1kg (2lb 4oz) watermelon

1 tbsp finely shredded mint

1 Place the lime juice in a small saucepan with the caster sugar. Stir over a low heat to dissolve the sugar, then boil for 1 minute or until reduced to a syrupy consistency. Pour into a jug and cool for 20 minutes, then refrigerate for 1 hour or overnight.

2 Cut the skin from the watermelon, then remove and discard the seeds. Cut the flesh into bite-size chunks, catching any juices in a bowl. Sprinkle the watermelon chunks with the mint and toss them together lightly.

3 Add the reserved melon juice to the chilled syrup and pour over the melon just before serving. Sprinkle with grated lime rind.

Imagine a long heatwave, then think of juicy chunks of watermelon coated in an ice-cold lime and mint syrup. It's almost too good to be true!

RASPBERRY YOGURT ICE

Serves 4

Calories 158

Fat 1g

Preparation 15 mins
plus 6 hrs freezing and 30
mins chilling

Simplicity

1 Place the raspberries in a food processor and blend until smooth, or use a hand blender. Press the mixture through a sieve into a bowl, discarding the pips, then add the sugar and mix well.

2 Mix in the raspberry yogurt and Greek yogurt. Pour the mixture into a shallow freezer container, cover, and freeze for 2 hours. Meanwhile, put a large empty bowl into the refrigerator to chill.

3 Spoon the raspberry mixture into the chilled bowl and beat with a fork or whisk until smooth to break down the ice crystals. Return to the container, cover, and freeze for a further 4 hours or until firm.

4 Transfer to the fridge for 30 minutes before serving to soften. Serve in scoops, decorated with fresh mint and raspberries.

350g (12oz) raspberries, defrosted if frozen

50g (2oz) caster sugar

300g (11oz) low fat raspberry yogurt

125g (4oz) virtually fat-free Greek yogurt

Fresh mint and raspberries to decorate

The unmistakable flavour of raspberries works really well in this tangy ice but there is nothing to stop you using fresh strawberries and strawberry yogurt instead.

SUMMER PUDDING WITH REDCURRANT SAUCE

Simplicity

Serves 6

Preparation 20 mins

plus 2-3 hrs chilling

Cooking 8 mins

Calories 177

Fat trace

1kg (2lb 4oz) fresh or frozen mixed berry fruits

3 tbsp caster sugar

8 slices white or wholemeal bread, crusts removed

2 tbsp redcurrant jelly

1 Place the fruit, sugar and 3 tablespoons of water in a saucepan and simmer for 5 minutes or until the fruit has softened. Leave to cool slightly.

2 Line the base and sides of a 900ml (1½ pint) pudding basin with 6 slices of the bread, cutting to fit and making sure there are no gaps. Strain the fruit, reserving the juice, then add the fruit to the basin. Cover with the remaining bread to form a lid. Spoon over 3-4 tablespoons of the reserved juice.

3 Place a plate on top of the bread, with a weight, such as a large can, on it. Place in the fridge for 2-3 hours to let the juices soak through the bread.

4 For the sauce, strain the reserved juice into a pan, stir in the redcurrant jelly and simmer for 2-3 minutes, until the jelly has all melted. Turn the pudding out on to a plate and serve with the sauce.

This is many people's favourite pudding – it's easy to make and healthy too. Instead of cream, try it with a spoonful of low fat plain or vanilla yogurt – you'll love it.

CHOCOLATE AND STRAWBERRY ROULADE

Serves 6

Calories 346

Fat 9g

Preparation 25 mins

Cooking 12 mins

plus 30 mins cooling

Simplicity

1 Preheat the oven to 200°C/400°F/Gas Mark 6. Grease a 33 x 23cm (13 x 9in) Swiss roll tin and line with non-stick baking paper. Whisk the eggs and sugar in a bowl over a pan of simmering water till pale and creamy. Take off the heat and whisk until cool.

2 Using a metal spoon, gently fold in the wholemeal flour into the mixture, then the white flour and cocoa with 1 tablespoon of hot water. Pour into the tin and smooth over with the back of a spoon. Bake for 10-12 minutes, until risen and firm. Turn out on to a sheet of non-stick baking paper, trim the sponge's edges with a knife and roll up with the paper inside. Place seam-side down on a wire rack to cool for 30 minutes. Then carefully unroll and discard the paper.

3 Mix together the yogurt and fromage frais and spread evenly over the cake with the strawberries. Roll up the cake and dust with cocoa and icing sugar.

Sunflower spread for greasing

3 medium eggs

125g (4oz) caster sugar

50g (2oz) plain wholemeal flour

50g (2oz) plain white flour, sifted

15g (½oz) cocoa powder, sifted, plus 2 tsp to dust

125g (4oz) Greek yogurt

100g (3½oz) virtually fat free fromage frais

150g (5oz) strawberries, sliced or chopped

Icing sugar to dust

This chocolate roulade may be in a low fat cookbook but it tastes divine. And if you get tired of strawberries, you can try fresh raspberries, sliced peaches, pears or bananas.

INDEX